SCOTLAND
THE LANDSCAPE BELOW

OVER 30
FULL COLOUR POSTCARDS

PARRAGON

3425
© 1993 Bramley Books
This edition published by Parragon Books
Printed and bound in Italy
All rights reserved
ISBN 1 85813 275 4
Front cover: Culzean Castle, Strathclyde
Title page: Glen Etive, Strathclyde
Back cover: Gleneagles Golf Course, Tayside

Dryburgh Abbey, Berwick, Borders

Brodick, Isle of Arran, Strathclyde

Anstruther, Fife

Dumfries, Dumfries and Galloway

Kelvingrove Park, Glasgow, Strathclyde

Edinburgh, Lothian

Scone Palace, Perth, Tayside

Perth, Tayside

Dundee, Tayside

Gleneagles Golf Course, Tayside

Floors Castle, Borders

Isle of Bute, Strathclyde

Inverness, Highland

Dumbarton, Strathclyde

Isle of Gigha, Strathclyde

Stirling Castle, Central Scotland

Abbotsford House, Roxburgh, Borders

Rhunahaorine Point, Isle of Kintyre, Strathclyde

Ailsa Craig, Strathclyde

Culzean Castle, Strathclyde

Glasgow, Strathclyde

Edinburgh Castle, Lothian

Forth Bridge, Firth of Forth

Tay Railway Bridge, Tayside

St. Andrews, Fife

Eildon Hills, Borders

Baile Mor, Isle of Iona, Strathclyde

Scaraster Bay, South Harris, Western Isles

Rothesay Bay, Isle of Bute, Strathclyde

Balmoral Castle, Grampian